ANYONE CAN BUILD A SPINNING WHEEL

W.C. West is a spinner and woodworker who built his first wheel for $1.98, using materials he found around the house. "All that's needed is a bit of woodworking skill, or lacking that, a strong desire to build your own spinning wheel for under $25." This book contains a complete materials list; clear large plans; three design variations; and simple instructions.

ANYONE CAN BUILD

A SPINNING WHEEL

by W.C. West

Robinson Township Public
Library District
606 N. Jefferson Street
Robinson, IL 62454

THRESH PUBLICATIONS

Copyright ©W.C.West 1975

All rights reserved. No part of this book may be reproduced or transmitted in any form or by any means, electronic or mechanical, including photocopying, recording or by any informational storage and retrieval system, without permission in writing from the publisher. Brief passages may be quoted for review purposes.

Printed in the United States of America

ISBN 0-913664-06-5

Thresh Publications
443 Sebastopol Avenue
Santa Rosa, CA 95401

Library of Congress Cataloging in Publication Data

West, Wilfred C   1912-1975
   Anyone can build a spinning wheel.

   1. Spinning-wheel.   I. Title.
TS1484.W47   681'.7677   75-12525
ISBN 0-913664-06-5

TO MY FAMILY

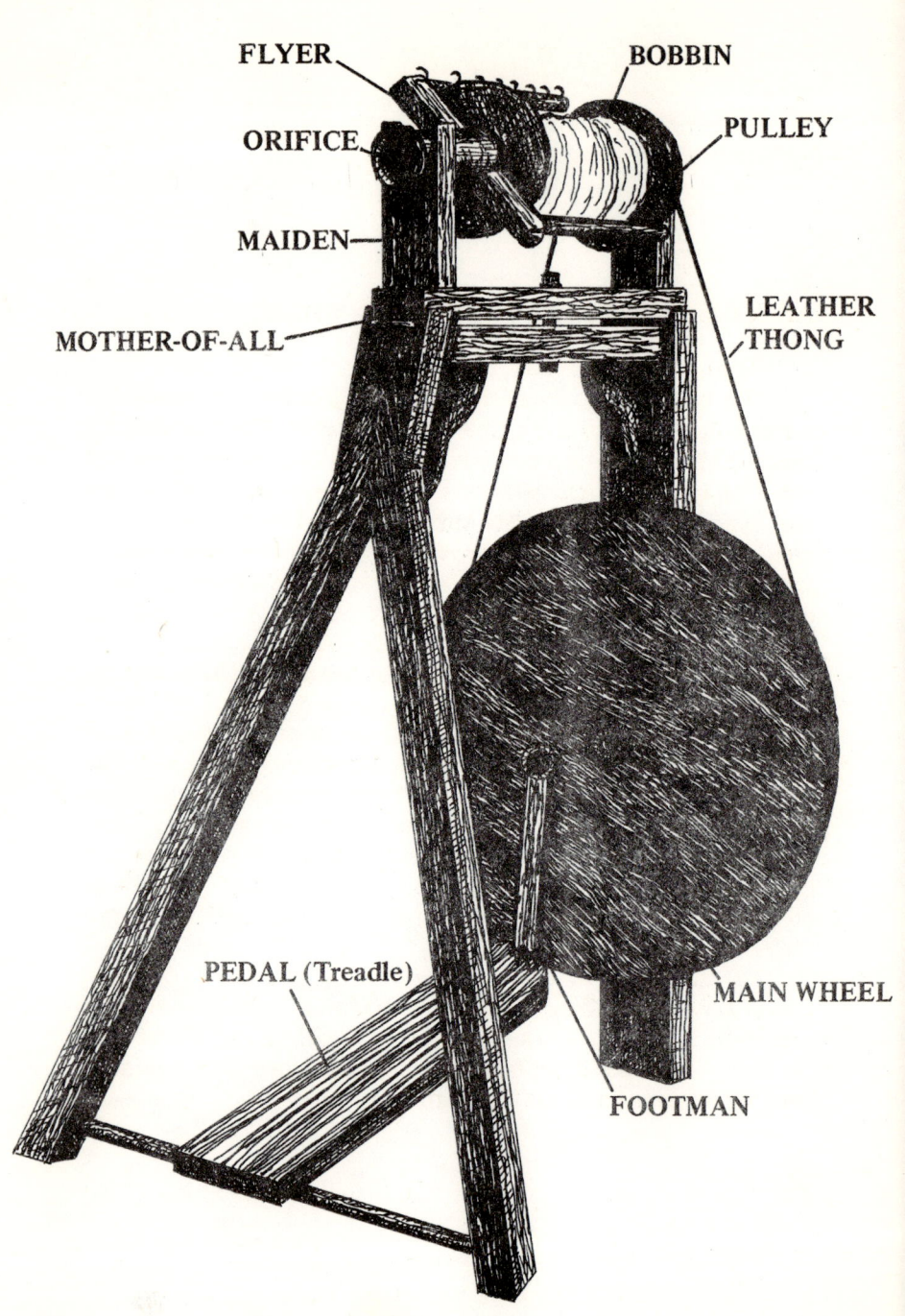

ANYONE CAN BUILD A SPINNING WHEEL

Well, nearly anyone!

To begin with, there is no law, regulation or reason for a spinning wheel to look like the wheel that Sleeping Beauty used, or the one Rumplestiltskin used. In fact, there are many other shapes and arrangements which have been used in the past which do not look like either of the familiar ones. The idea behind it all is that you want to twist the fibers into a yarn and then wind them up for storage. The spinning wheel built from the plans given here will do the work, but does not look quite like the ones in the story books.

This spinning wheel is simple in design and appearance, and is easy to construct. All that's needed is a bit of woodworking skill, or lacking that, a strong desire to build your own spinning wheel for under $25. The drawings all have the dimensions printed on them and there is usually more than one view of the same piece to make it easy to visualize. Some spinning terms are used, as are names of processes, materials and manipulations in woodworking. These I try to make as clear as I can, so that persons unversed in craftwork can understand.

A minimum of tools are needed. If you have access to power tools, use them, things will go faster, but they are not required. I used some power tools in building my wheel, but on most of it, hand tools were used to be sure they could be used by anyone to make the parts.

TOOLS YOU WILL NEED:
- Coping saw with extra blades (you could also use an electric saber saw or shop jigsaw)
- Hammer
- Hand drill with kit of graduated size drill bits
- Hand saw
- Plane (not absolutely needed)
- Try square (not absolutely needed)
- Sandpaper (assorted grit package)
- Rule (yardstick, flexible tape)
- Pencil
- Screwdriver
- Pliers
- Workbench (sturdy table, sawhorse, packing crate, etc.)
- Vise (handy, but not absolutely needed)
- Hacksaw
- File
- Knife for whittling (keep it sharp!)
- Soldering iron, solder (plain), tinner's acid
  - or
- Propane torch — all soldered joints would be better either silver soldered or brazed
- Allen wrench to fit 8-32 and an 8-32 tap and handle (for Va only)

MATERIALS YOU WILL NEED:
- 1 piece of 1/4" plywood, 1' x 4', for main wheel (the bobbin ends and bobbin pulley come from the waste after cutting out main wheel).
- 3 dowels, 1 each – 1/4", 3/8", 1/2" – all 36" long
- 1 package 3/4" brads or wire nails
- 1 large dowel or clothes pole, 3" long and 1-1/2" diameter (for orifice)
- 1 steel rod 1/4" x 12" (8" needed for spindle, balance for alignment)
- 1 piece wood 1" x 2-1/4" x 20-1/2" (for back leg, all views)

8 cup hooks (I found some 3/8" hooks that were just right)
1 piece wood 9/16" x 3/4" x 5" (in detail F and G)
1 piece wood 1-1/2" x 3/4" x 20" (for M, N, O, side view as assembled at detail L)
1 piece wood 3/8" x 3/4" x 5-1/2" (detail T)
1 piece wood 3/4" x 2-1/4" x 15" (treadle U)
1 piece wood 1/2" x 1/2" x 6" (for U latch assembly)
2 bolts, 4" and 3" 1/4-20 (all variations except Va)
3 washers, 1/4"
2 leather washers, 1" diameter, 1/4" hole
2 nuts, 1/4" x 20
2 cotter pins, 1/16"
1 piece pipe, 1/4" inside diameter, 1-1/4" long (outside diameter whatever it is)
1 carriage bolt, 1/4", washer and wingnut, 2-1/2" long
2 RH wood screws, 3/4" (for main wheel except in design Va)
1 RH wood screw, 1" (treadle latch pivot)
2 RH wood screws, 1/2" (for W/1 or W/2 only)
8 RH wood screws, 3/4" (for Va main wheel bearing pieces only)
3 setscrews, 8-32 Allen
White glue
1 piece plywood, 3/4" x 15" x 24" (for designs W/1 and W/2 only)
1 piece wood, 1" x 1" x 4' (for design W only)
Scrap wood for bracing blocks
Lead (old wheel weights, old printing type, telephone sheathing, etc.)
Tuna fish can (use for melting lead, hold with pliers)
Your imagination for anything else you think you need that I haven't listed.

INSTRUCTIONS

Instructions — read through all of the directions before starting — some of the steps will be clearer if you know what's coming up next. When you have done this, read through again.

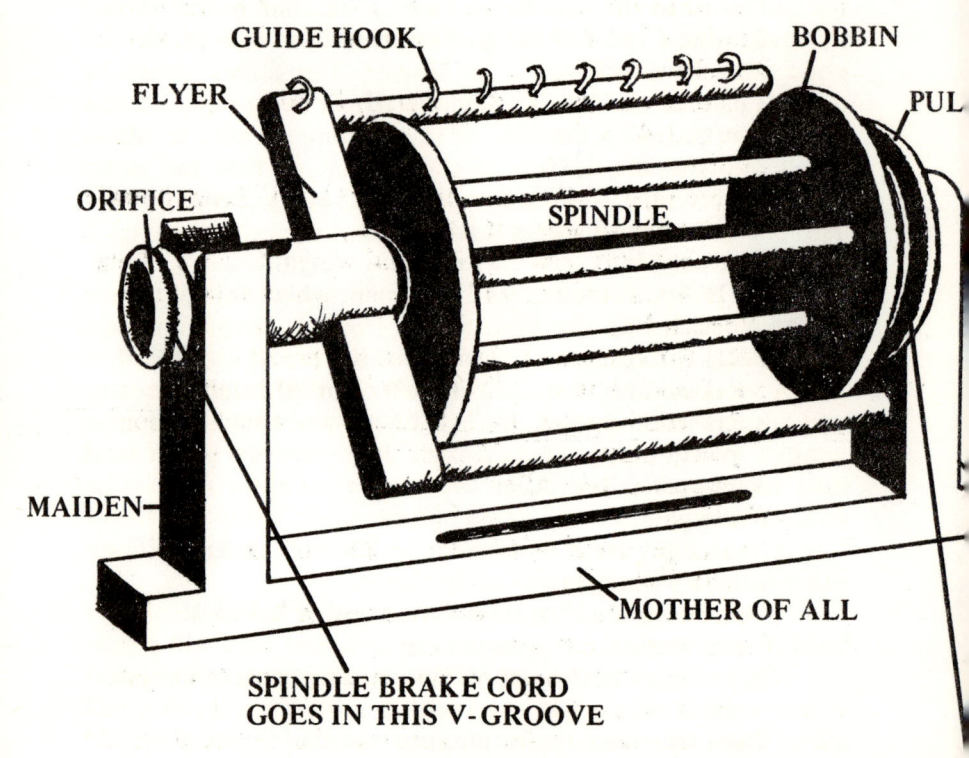

Figures A, B, C, D, and E in the drawings show the pulley (whorl) and the bobbin (a kind of spool) which is driven by a belt from the main wheel. On some spinning wheels the pulley is part of the bobbin, but in this design I thought people would like one or more extra bobbins so they could continue to spin when the first one became filled. Merely replace the full bobbin with an empty one and put the pulley onto the spindle and go ahead. The pulley shown is smaller than the bobbin in diameter. If it were made the same size, it would run a bit slower. The pulley could be made a part of the bobbin and the whole thing replaced as a unit when changing bobbins. If this is done, be sure to adjust the lengthwise dimensions of the bobbin so that the outer length is the same as the separate bobbin and pulley together. The two-part design uses a leather washer as a spacer on each end of the bobbin.

The pulley is made using a coping saw to cut the three plywood circles to the dimensions given. A simple compass for drawing the circles can be made of a piece of cardboard or a thin wooden slat. Put a small brad or pin through the strip and measure out one and one-half inches and drill a hole large enough to put a pencil tip through. Just press the pin or brad into the wood at the place chosen for a center and scribe around this point with your home-made compass. Don't forget that one circle is smaller by one-half inch. Make another hole in your compass accordingly.

When using a coping saw care must be taken to always hold it so a vertical cut is made, else a sloped edge will result.

These three circles are drilled in the center (the point where your compass nail was) with a hole diameter that will allow them to rotate freely on your spindle. A small rat tail file carefully used will open the 1/4" hole, or a small piece of sandpaper rolled up and drawn a few times through will do the trick. Sand these circles well and slip them on a scrap piece of steel the diameter of your spindle. Apply glue between all surfaces (I used a white glue like Elmer's) and nail the sandwich together with brads, being sure they are properly aligned to be true on the shaft. There is another hole shown on the drawings; this is to be drilled as located, then a small piece of wooden dowel glued into it. This small dowel fits into the hole in the end of the bobbin to drive it.

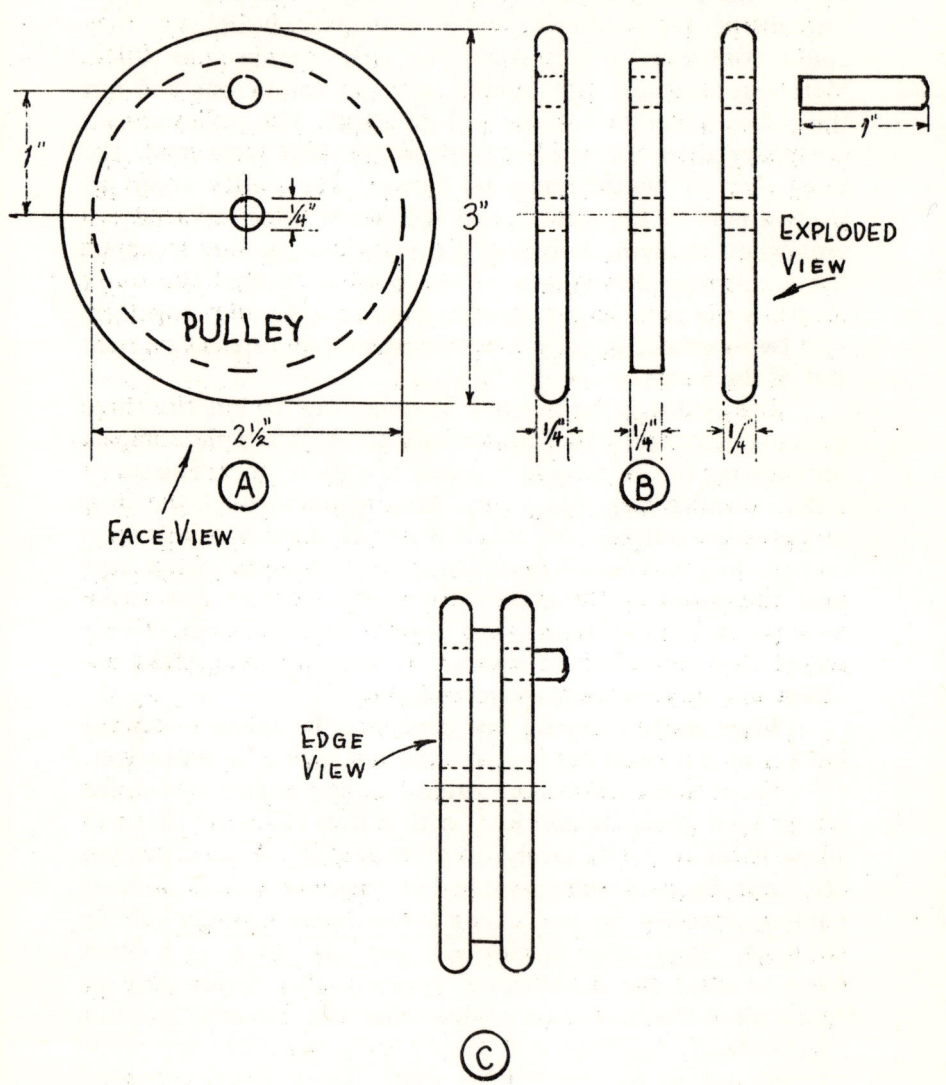

Figures D and E show the end and side views of the bobbin. As with the pulley, the bobbin ends are two discs sawed from quarter-inch plywood. They are drilled as indicated and fitted together with the four dowels as shown in the drawings. In E, only two dowels can be seen as the other two are behind the visible ones. Use quarter-inch metal rod while the glue is still wet to align the spool so it is even.

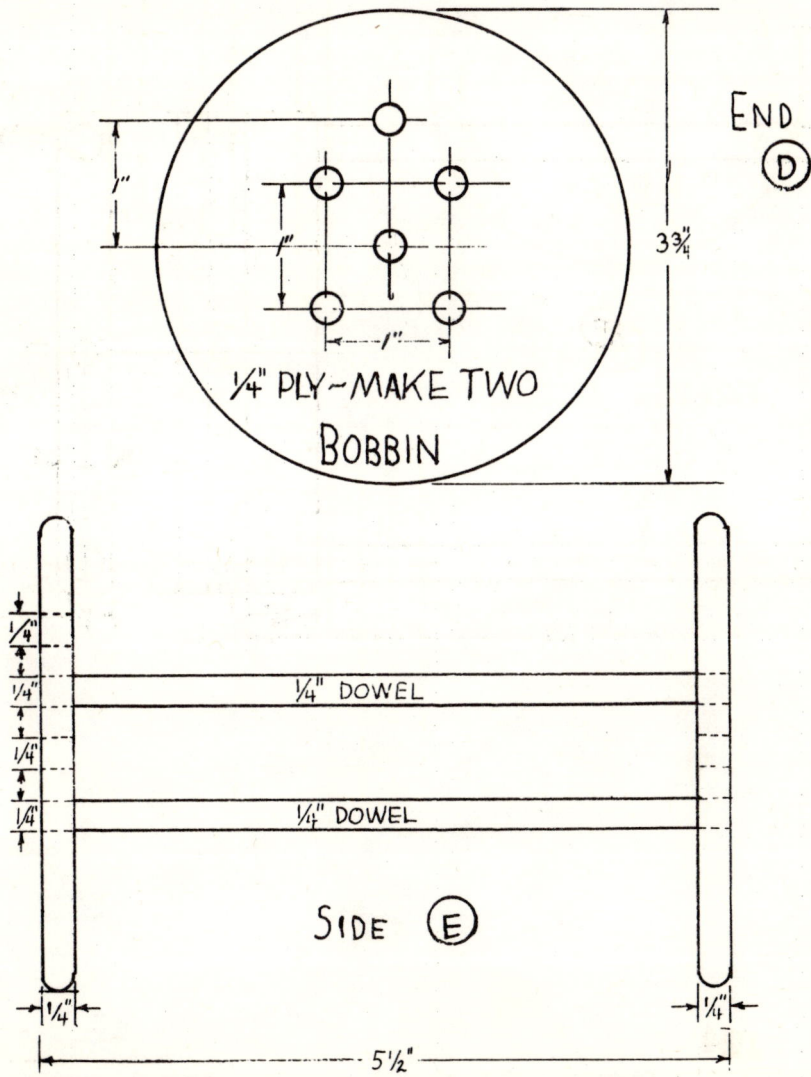

Figures F and G show part of the flyer (the gizmo on the spinning wheel which rotates around the bobbin with the guide hooks on one arm).

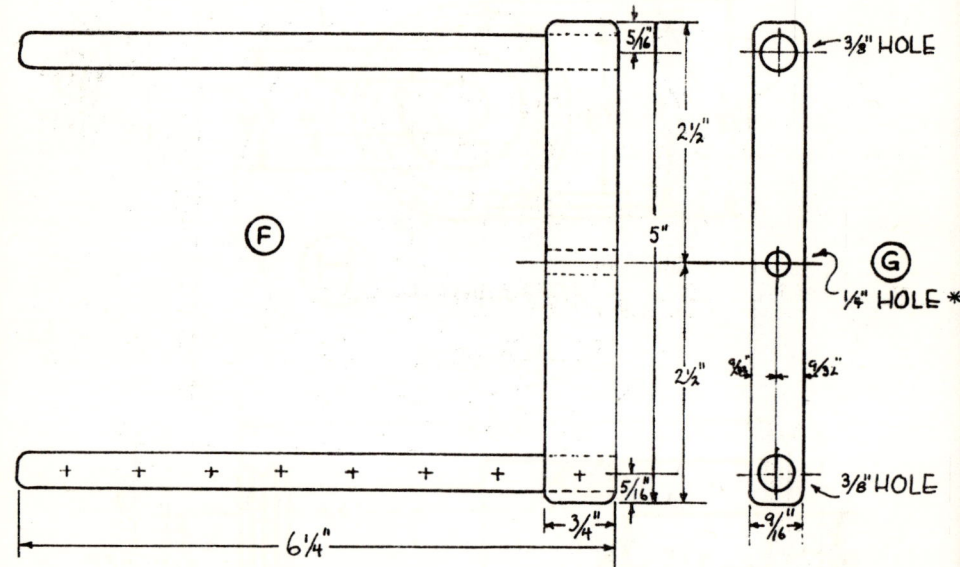

Figures H and I show the orifice through which the yarn is spun.

The part indicated by H and I can be whittled from pine or any other wood you can manage to cut. If you have a friend with a wood lathe, perhaps you could flatter him into making this part on his lathe. If you have such a friend, don't stop here, you might save yourself some hand work if you let him see the drawings and help you on the more tedious circular cut parts.

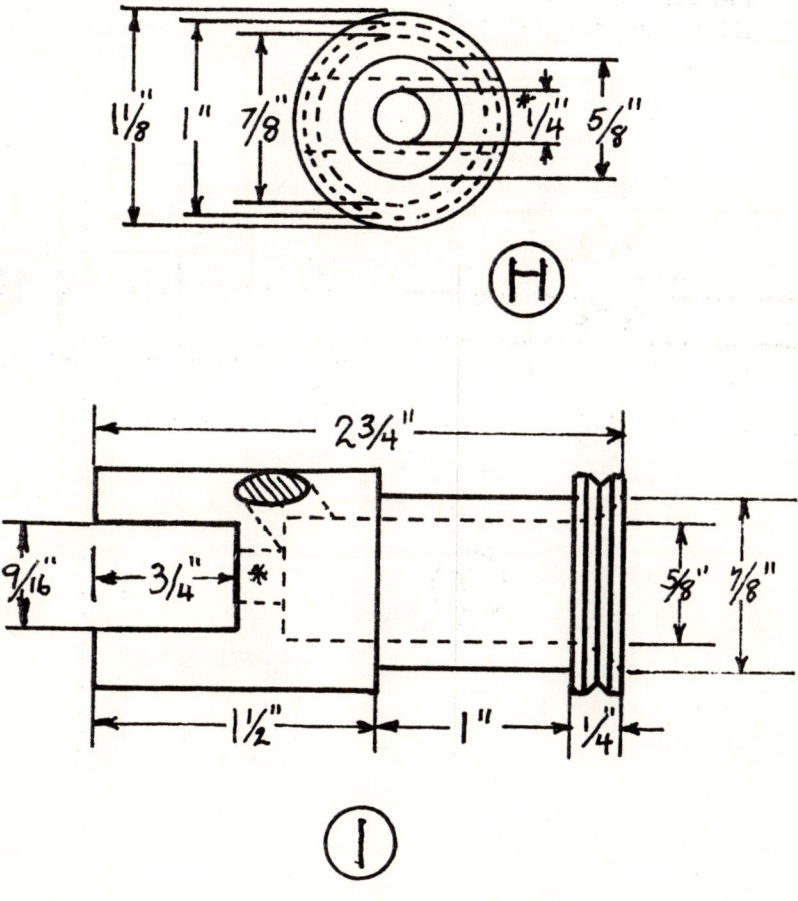

Figure J is the metal spindle which is filed square for one inch and, when F and H are assembled by gluing, is driven into both at the hole marked with an asterisk. (The asterisk is to caution you against drilling this hole too large.) Try your drill out on a scrap and see how the square end fits before drilling the flyer. For that matter, try all your holes out in a piece of scrap before drilling the various holes. You'll find that there will be fewer mistakes as to size, and things will fit and run better.

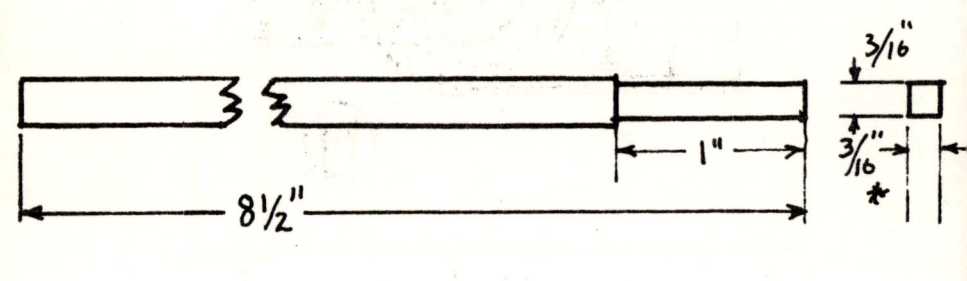

Figure K shows the flyer as it will look assembled. Guide hooks go at the crosses as shown on one dowel in Figure F.

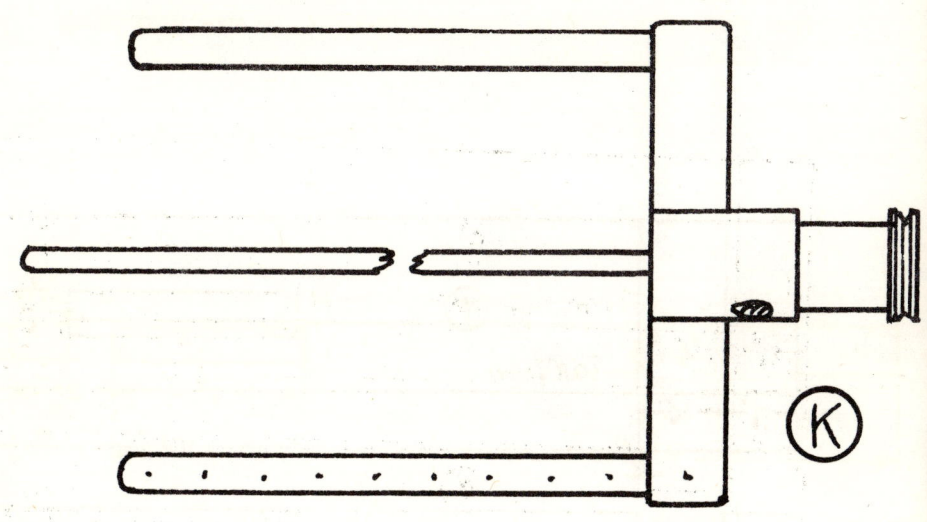

If you have an old pedal-type sewing machine, drop the head (if it drops) or take it out and set it aside. Make a piece of plywood to fit where the machine head sat. On this, fix a sort of bridge to elevate your spinning head so the sewing machine belt will drive it. Pattern this bridge after the top part of the spinning wheel frame as shown in the drawings, but don't necessarily slant the front. You're home free and all set to spin as of now. You can skip the rest of the construction and congratulate yourself on being so smart as to have that old treadle sewing machine.

Figure L shows how the next piece looks when assembled. The verticals on an old-timer wheel would be called Maidens, while the flat piece which holds them would be the Mother-of-All. Figures M/1, M/2, N/1, O/2 and N/2 are various views of the pieces for Figure L. The small peg can be whittled in any shape and just plugged into the hole in the lower portion of O/1. It is for the spindle brake cord.

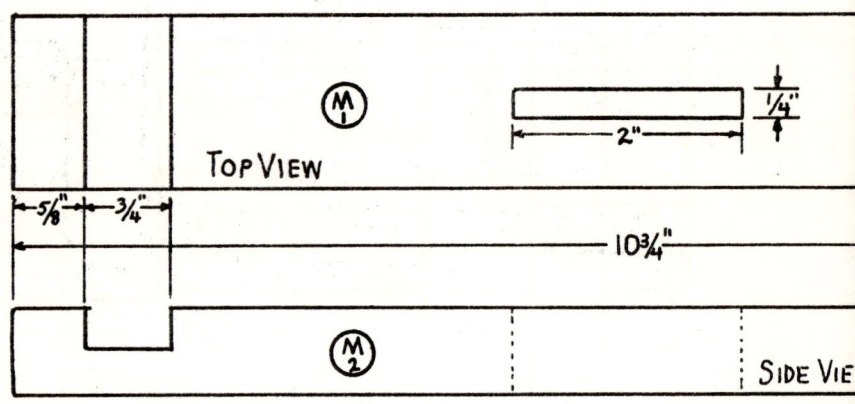

Robinson Township Public
Library District
606 N. Jefferson Street
Robinson, IL 62454

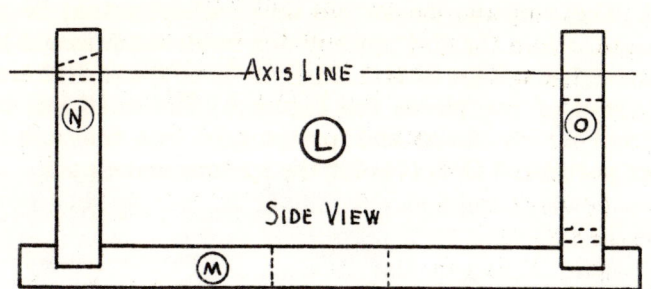

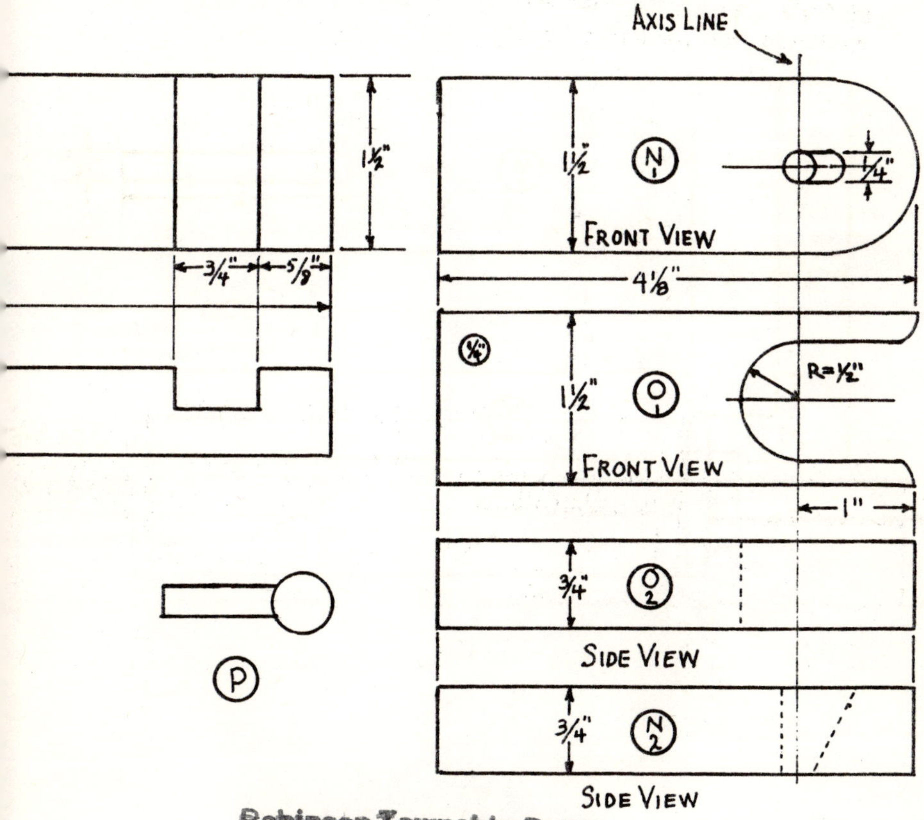

Figure Q is the axle shaft for the large drive wheel. It is made by sawing the head off a bolt with a hacksaw. File the end smooth and run a nut up the threads, adding a plain washer. This will be inserted in the hole you'll drill later in the back leg. Another washer and nut will hold this in place. Near the end of the smooth part a 1/16 inch hole should be drilled to take a cotter pin. Three inches did fine for mine, but your wheel and back leg may be thicker, so get a bolt the length you need.

Figure R is a similar axle, handled the same way. It is for the top end of the footman (in mechanical parlance, a pitman arm; in layman's language, just the stick which connects the foot pedal to the crank pin on the wheel).

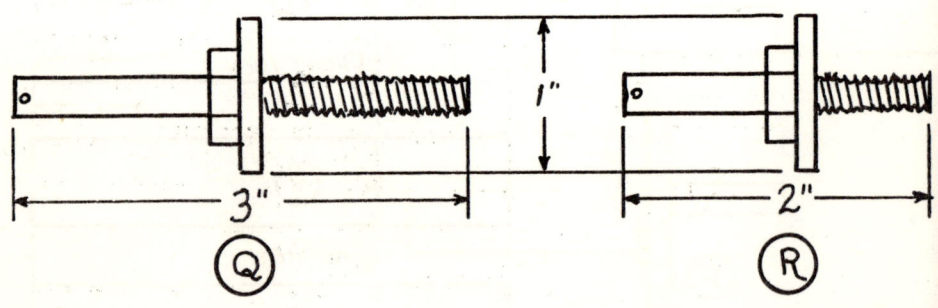

Your do-it-yourself friend who helped with the orifice may also have some of the tools, equipment and know-how to help you on the metal sawing and soldering. Or, perhaps your friendly neighborhood gas station shop man, or the local garage could be persuaded to drill a few holes and solder a few pieces of metal for you.

S/1 and S/2 are the main bearing, a piece of pipe on which there is a washer soldered. The outer size is not important. The inner dimension should turn freely but not sloppily on the 1/4 inch axle bolt. The washer has two additional holes into which small screws are fitted into the wheel, making it solid with the wheel.

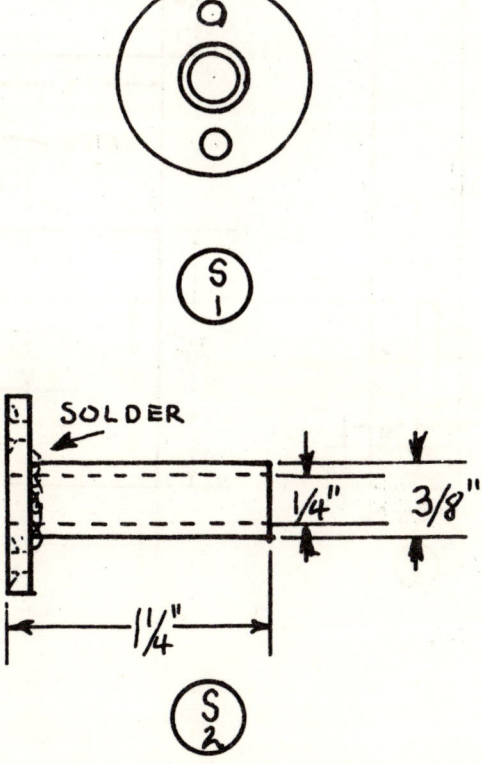

T/1 and T/2 are the footman (mentioned above). U/1 and U/2 are side and bottom views of the foot pedal (treadle). The circular part marked "1" is the 1/2 inch dowel on the front legs on which the pedal pivots. Number "3" is a latch. When you drill the hole in the top end on the footman, wobble the stick so the outer edges of the hole become larger than that part in the center, because the stick must wobble a bit and needs the clearance. The bottom of this footman is fixed to the pedal with a leather thong.

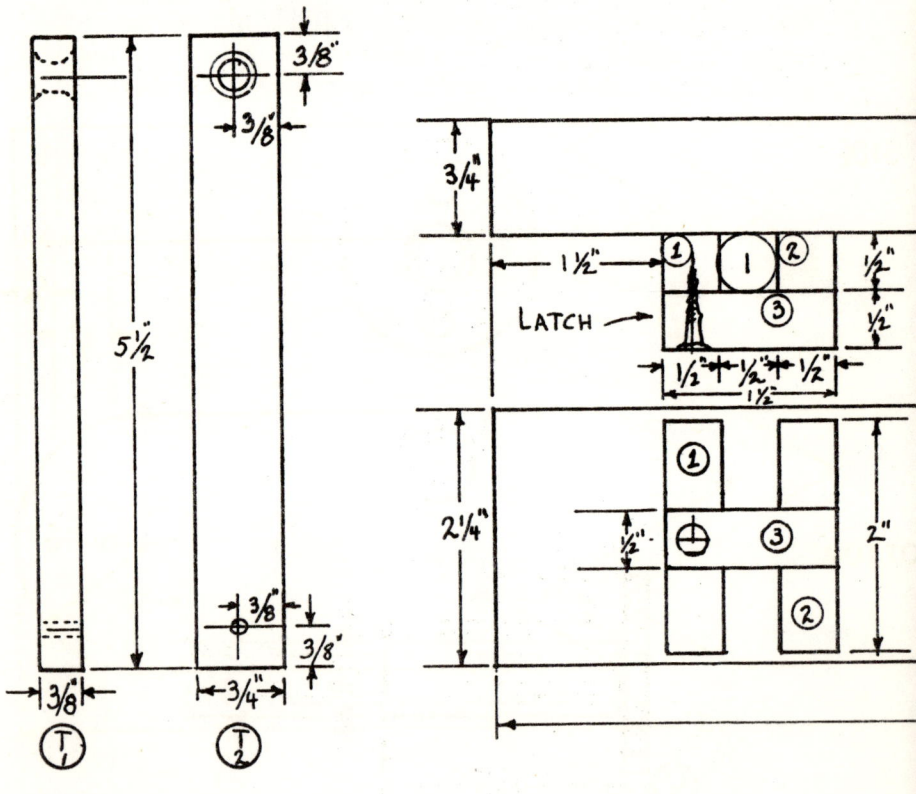

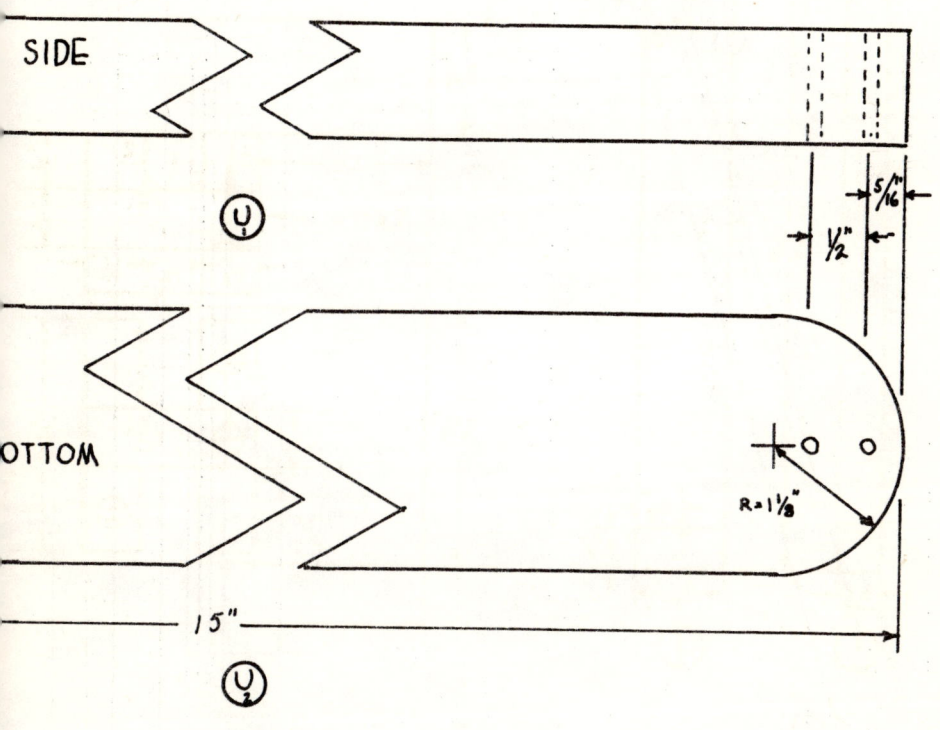

Figure V is the side view of the frame. This shows the main wheel which is made in a manner similar to the bobbin pulley — three discs of 1/4 inch plywood, glued and bradded together and drilled as indicated in the drawings.

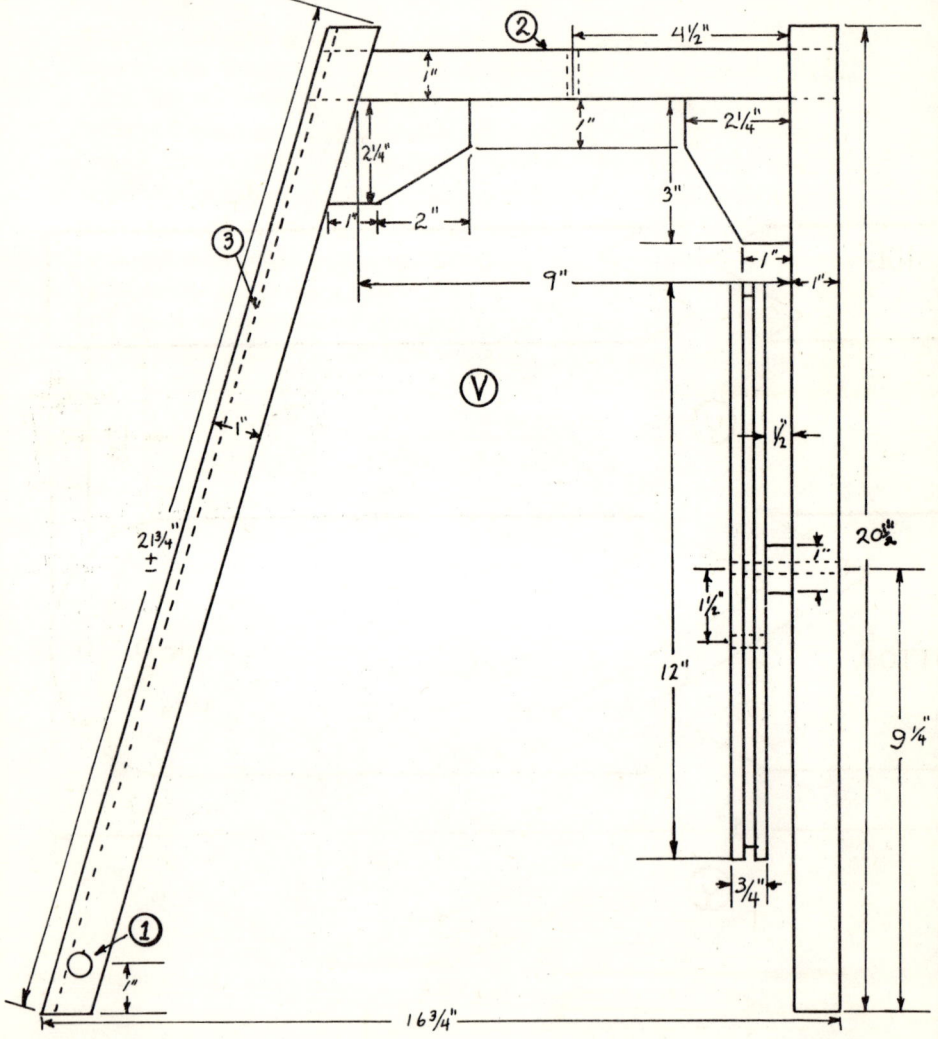

A hardware store yardstick makes a very handy large compass for scribing the large circles. A small brad in one end and a small hole or holes at the radii you want. Put the tip of a pencil in the small hole and around you go. Don't make the mistake of putting the brad at the 1 inch mark and using the 6 inch mark for your 12 inch circles. They will come out only 10 inches.

The main wheel is weighted to gain a flywheel effect. When making the main wheel, assemble the back and center pieces and drill the holes around the outer edge for the lead. Assemble the front face of the wheel before bouring the lead. These holes should be large as indicated in drawing X and could be as large as one and a quarter inches in diameter. Bend one side of the rim of a tuna fish can to form a grip for your pliers. Form a pouring spout on the other side. Melt the lead in the clean dry can over low heat. Pour lead in the holes after driving a brad crosswise into each hole to anchor the lead. The circle of holes is made near the rim to get the weight as far out as possible.

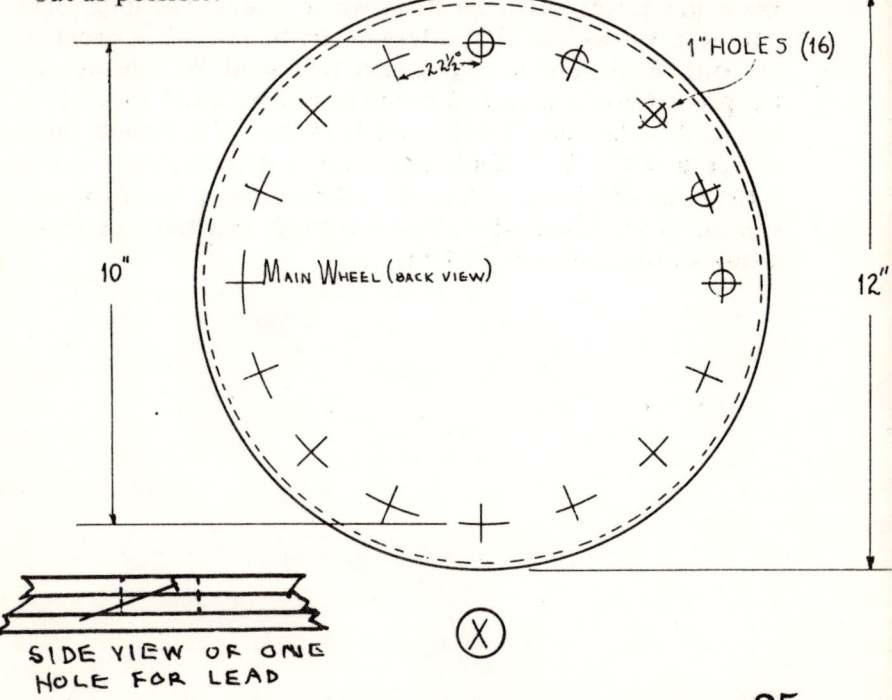

SIDE VIEW OF ONE HOLE FOR LEAD

In Figure V, 1 is the position of the pedal pivot dowel; 2 is the part where the Mother-of-All sits. A quarter inch carriage bolt, head up, projects through and a wingnut and washer are on the bottom. This serves two purposes: first, to position the head forward or backward to align the drive cord with the two pulleys; and second, to allow loosening enough to shove wedges in front and back to take up and adjust cord tension. Number 3 shows the front leg face if three-quarter inch plywood is used for the alternate design. Keep in mind that the front legs are tilted and therefore longer (about 21¾ inches) so it is best to make the bottom end a bit longer and trim off the bottom to where the top horizontal base is level. Use a spacer (a piece of plywood, cardboard or washers) between the wheel and the back leg. Mine was an additional ½ inch piece of plywood, about two inches in diameter, glued to the wheel.

Figure W is the front view of the frame. The legs are one inch square wood, and the top part of the front legs was made from the pieces cut from them when making the long taper cut. W/1 shows the first alternate frame, which is easier to saw out. W/2 could be coping-sawed by hand. W/3 shows that the pivot dowel is attached to the rear of the front legs, which means that the pedal must be made shorter. The treadle pivot dowel in detail W/3 should have flats cut on each end where it fits to legs of frame W/1 or W/2. Before fixing together with screws, dab a bit of white glue on dowel end flats, then put in the screws and draw up tight.

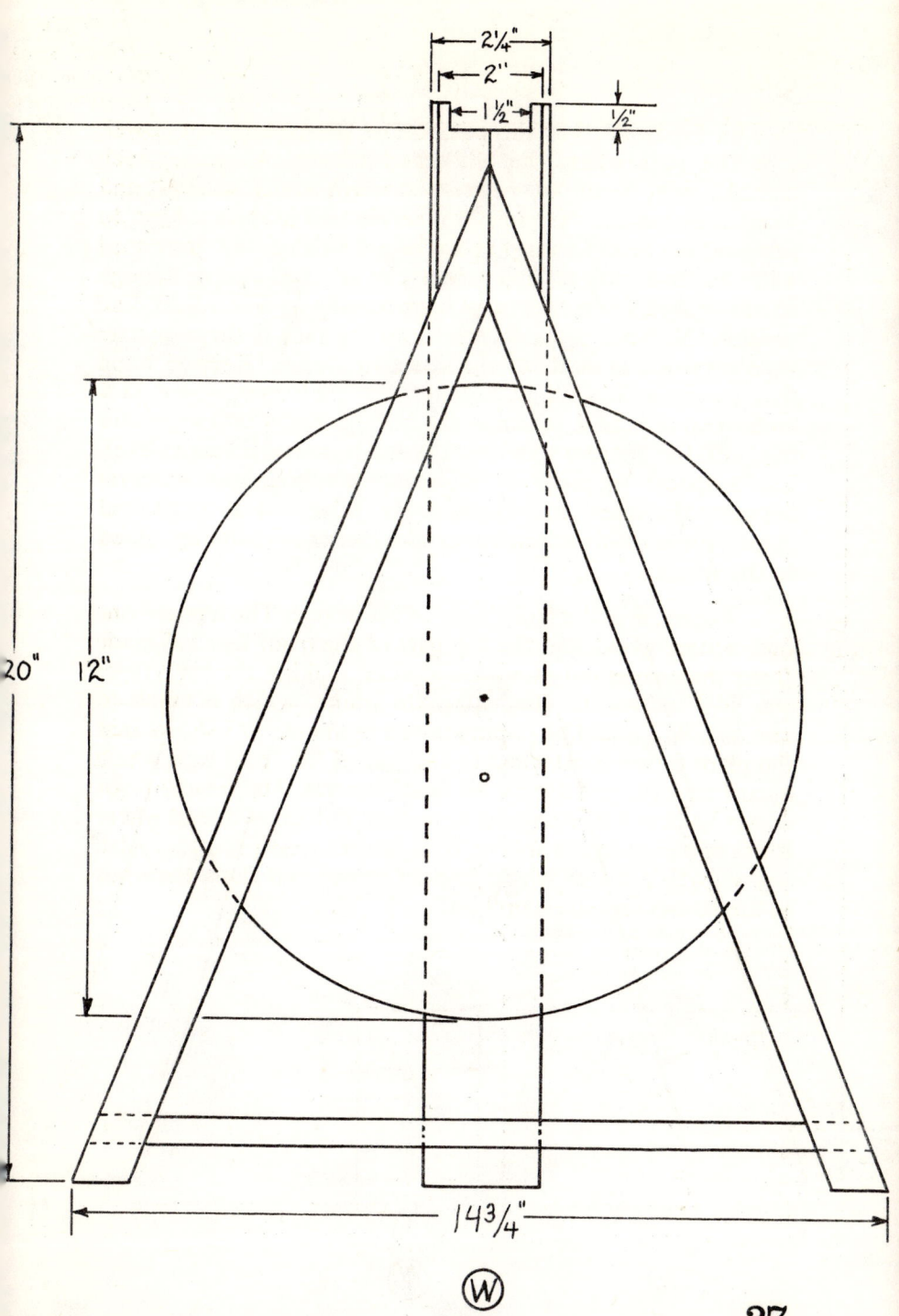

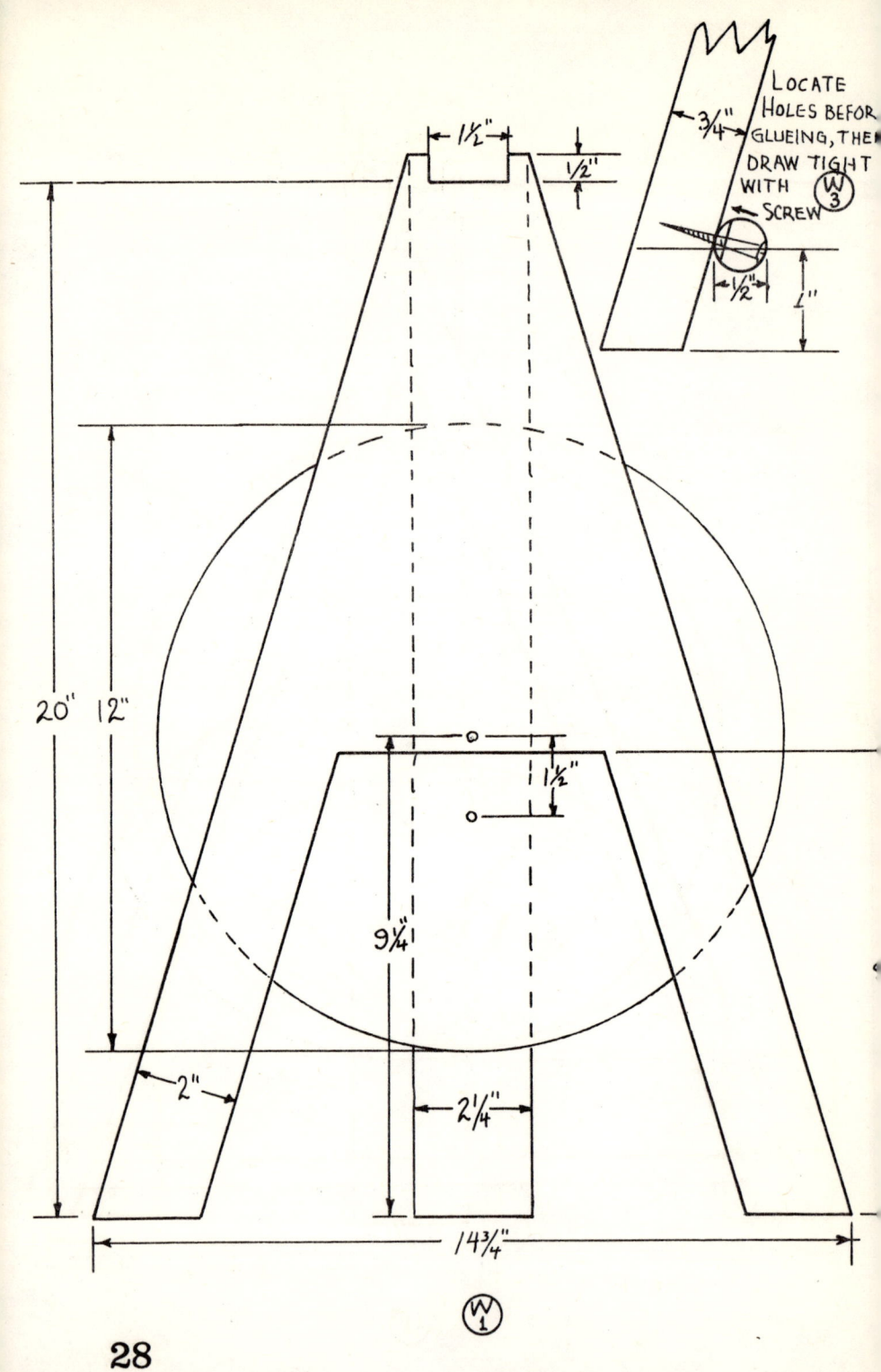

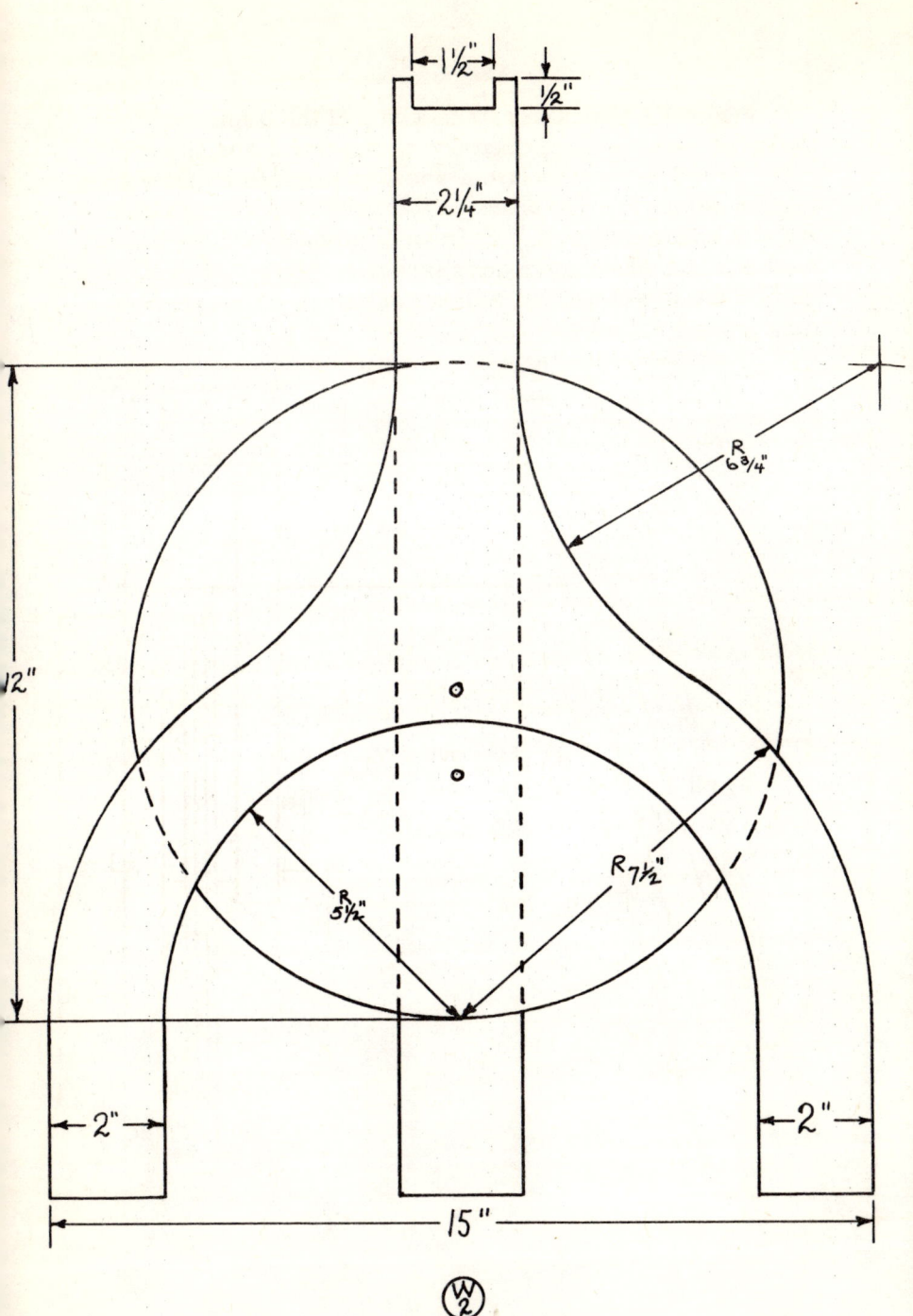

Figure Va is an alternate handling of the frame, wherein the wheel axle is fixed securely to the wheel and the additional wooden member from the top crosspiece added to make a second bearing piece for this axle. The bracing blocks are also changed to suit. This frame is probably a more stable method. The wheel and axle as shown in Figure V does allow quite a bit of wobble, but it does not seem to affect the spinning process when I use it.

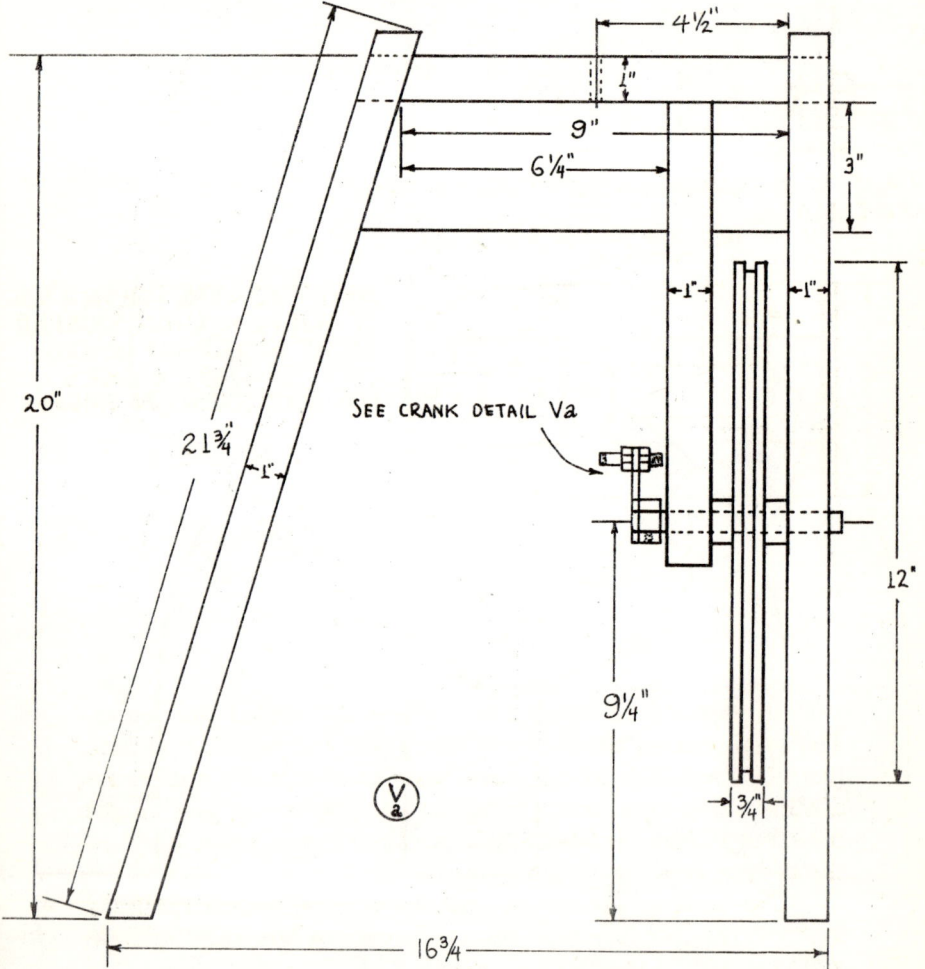

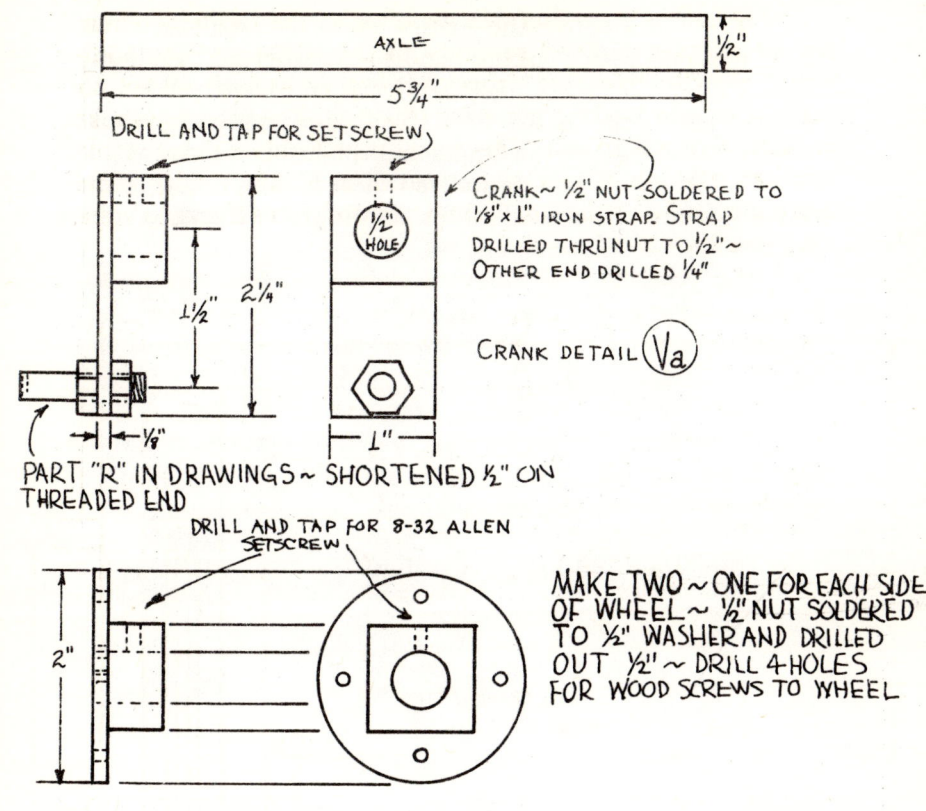

In assembling the frame, I glued and nailed the pieces. The small corner blocks were also glued and nailed. Old-time practice probably would have been to drill holes and insert dowels along with face gluing. Later, screws and glue might have been used by wheel-makers. Take your choice and use the system which best suits you.

The hole in the bobbin may have to be enlarged slightly so that the bobbin will rotate freely on the steel spindle which is part of the flyer.

The V-groove on the orifice piece of the flyer is for a cord, attached with a rubber band to the whittled peg, looped around the orifice piece and then fastened to the peg or a nail or what have you. On my first wheel, there was enough space between the edge of the frame and the head so that the cord could be drawn down and wedged therein. You might be able to do this too. You must be able to undo one end to adjust the tension.

Cut your leather thong or sewing machine belt so that it fits snugly around the large wheel and the pulley wheel. Fasten it around the wheels by sewing the ends together or by using the metal clip that comes with the belt.

Light oil can be used to lubricate all bearings. A bit of oil on the flyer orifice bearing and brake groove helps too. Don't get varnish, paint or stain on either of the latter two pieces, as they will get hot and bind.

Good luck and happy spinning.